The Touch of You

THE TOUCH OF YOU

Amy Lowell's Poems

of Love and Beauty

Selected by Peter Seymour

Illustrated by Bill Greer

♛ HALLMARK EDITIONS

THE TOUCH OF YOU

OPAL

You are ice and fire,
The touch of you burns my hands like snow.
You are cold and flame.
You are the crimson of amaryllis,
The silver of moon-touched magnolias.
When I am with you,
My heart is a frozen pond
Gleaming with agitated torches.

A SHOWER

That sputter of rain, flipping the hedge-rows
And making the highways hiss.
How I love it!
And the touch of you upon my arm
As you press against me that my umbrella
May cover you.

Tinkle of drops on stretched silk.
Wet murmur through green branches.

JULY MIDNIGHT

Fireflies flicker in the tops of trees,
Flicker in the lower branches,
Skim along the ground.
Over the moon-white lilies
Is a flashing and ceasing of small, lemon-green
        stars.
As you lean against me,
Moon-white,
The air all about you
Is slit, and pricked, and pointed with sparkles
        of lemon-green flame
Starting out of a background of vague, blue trees.

TO-MORROW TO FRESH WOODS
AND PASTURES NEW

As for a moment he stands, in hardy
    masculine beauty,
Poised on the fircrested rock, over
    the pool which below him
Gleams in the wavering sunlight, waiting
    the shock of his plunging.
So for a moment I stand, my feet planted
    firm in the present,
Eagerly scanning the future which is so
    soon to possess me.

from IN EXCELSIS

How has the rainbow fallen upon my heart?
How have I snared the seas to lie in my fingers
And caught the sky to be a cover for my head?
How have you come to dwell with me,
Compassing me with the four circles of your mystic
    lightness,
So that I say "Glory! Glory!" and bow before you
As to a shrine?

Do I tease myself that morning is morning
    and a day after?
Do I think the air a condescension,
The earth a politeness,
Heaven a boon deserving thanks?
So you—air—earth—heaven—
I do not thank you,
I take you,
I live .
And those things which I say in consequence
Are rubies mortised in a gate of stone.

OBLIGATION

Hold your apron wide
That I may pour my gifts into it,
So that scarcely shall your two arms hinder them
From falling to the ground.
I would pour them upon you
And cover you,
For greatly do I feel this need
Of giving you something,
Even these poor things.

Dearest of my Heart!

BULLION

My thoughts
Chink against my ribs
And roll about like silver hail-stones.
I should like to spill them out,
And pour them, all shining,
Over you.
But my heart is shut upon them
And holds them straitly.

Come, You! and open my heart;
That my thoughts torment me no longer,
But glitter in your hair.

WINTER'S TURNING

Snow is still on the ground,
But there is a golden brightness in the air.
Across the river,
Blue,
Blue,
Sweeping widely under the arches
Of many bridges,
Is a spire and a dome,
Clear as though ringed with ice-flakes,
Golden, and pink, and jocund.
On a near-by steeple,
A golden weather-cock flashes smartly,
His open beak "Cock-a-doodle-dooing"
Straight at the ear of Heaven.
A tall apartment house,
Crocus-coloured,
Thrusts up from the street
Like a new-sprung flower.
Another street is edged and patterned
With the bloom of bricks,
Houses and houses of rose-red bricks,
Every window a-glitter.
The city is a parterre,
Blowing and glowing,
Alight with the wind,

                              Washed over

Washed over with gold and mercury.
Let us throw up our hats,
For we are past the age of balls
And have none handy.
Let us take hold of hands,
And race along the sidewalks,
And dodge the traffic in crowded streets.
Let us whir with the golden spoke-wheels
Of the sun.
For to-morrow Winter drops
    into the waste-basket,
And the calendar calls it March.

THE PEDDLER OF FLOWERS

I came from the country
With flowers,
Larkspur and roses,
Fretted lilies
In their leaves,
And long, cool lavender.

I carried them
From house to house,
And cried them
Down hot streets.
The sun fell
Upon my flowers,
And the dust of the streets
Blew over my basket.
That night
I slept upon the open seats
Of a circus,
Where all day long
People had watched
The antics
Of a painted clown.

ΔΙΨΑ

Look, Dear, how bright the moonlight is to-night!
See where it casts the shadow of that tree
Far out upon the grass. And every gust
Of light night wind comes laden with the scent
Of opening flowers which never bloom by day:
Night-scented stocks, and four-o'clocks, and that
Pale yellow disk, upreared on its tall stalk,
The evening primrose, comrade of the stars.
It seems as though the garden which you love
Were like a swinging censer, its incense
Floating before us as a reverent act
To sanctify and bless our night of love.
Tell me once more you love me, that 'tis you
Yes, really you, I touch, so, with my hand;
And tell me it is by your own free will
That you are here, and that you like to be
Just here, with me, under this sailing pine.
I need to hear it often for my heart
Doubts naturally, and finds it hard to trust.
Ah, Dearest, you are good to love me so,
And yet I would not have it goodness, rather
Excess of selfishness in you to need
Me through and through, as flowers need the sun.
I wonder can it really be that you
And I are here alone, and that the night
Is full of hours, and all the world asleep,

And none can call to you to come away;
For you have given all yourself to me
Making me gentle by your willingness.
Has your life too been waiting for this time,
Not only mine the sharpness of this joy?
Dear Heart, I love you, worship you as though
I were a priest before a holy shrine.
I'm glad that you are beautiful, although
Were you not lovely still I needs must love;
But you are all things, it must have been so
For otherwise it were not you. Come, close;
When you are in the circle of my arm
Faith grows a mountain and I take my stand
Upon its utmost top. Yes, yes, once more
Kiss me, and let me feel you very near
Wanting me wholly, even as I want you.
Have years behind been dark? Will those to come
Bring unguessed sorrows into our two lives?
What does it matter, we have had to-night!
To-night will make us strong, for we believe
Each in the other, this is a sacrament.
Beloved, is it true?

LOVE NOTES

A Lover

If I could catch the green lantern of the firefly
I could see to write you a letter.

To a Husband

Brighter than fireflies upon the Uji River
Are your words in the dark, Beloved.

Ephemera

Silver-green lanterns tossing among windy branches:
So an old man thinks
Of the loves of his youth.

The Return

Coming up from my boat
In haste to lighten your anxiety,
I saw, reflected in the circular metal mirror,
The face and hands of a woman
Arranging her hair.

From a Window

Your footfalls on the drum bridge beside my house
Are like the pattering drops of a passing shower,
So soon are they gone.

A Burnt Offering

Because there was no wind,
The smoke of your letters hung in the air
For a long time;
And its shape
Was the shape of your face,
My Beloved.

Prime

Your voice is like bells over roofs at dawn
When a bird flies
And the sky changes to a fresher colour.

Speak, speak, Beloved.
Say little things
For my ears to catch
And run with them to my heart.

from MAY EVENING IN CENTRAL PARK

Lines of lamp-light
Splinter the black water,
And all through
The dim park
Are lamps
Hanging among the trees.
But they are only like fireflies
Pricking the darkness,
And I lean my body against it
And spread out my fingers
To let it drift through them.
I am a swimmer
In the damp night,
Or a bird
Floating over the sucking grasses.
I am a lover
Tracking the silver foot-prints
Of the moon.
I am a young man,
In Central Park,
With Spring
Bursting over me.

GENERATIONS

You are like the stem
Of a young beech-tree,
Straight and swaying,
Breaking out in golden leaves.
Your walk is like the blowing of a beech-
     tree
On a hill.
Your voice is like leaves
Softly struck upon by a South wind.
Your shadow is no shadow, but a scat-
     tered sunshine;
And at night you pull the sky down
     to you
And hood yourself in stars.

But I am like a great oak under a cloudy
     sky,
Watching a stripling beech grow up
     at my feet.

ENTENTE CORDIALE

The young gentleman from the foreign
    nation
Sat on the sofa and smiled.
He stayed for two hours and I talked
    to him.
He answered agreeably,
He was very precise, very graceful, very
    enthusiastic.
I thought:
Is it possible that there are no nations,
    only individuals?
That it is the few who give gold
    and flowers,
While the many have only copper
So worn that even the stamp is obliter-
    ated?
I talked to the young gentleman from
    the foreign nation,
And the faint smell of copper assailed my
    nostrils:
Copper,
Twisted copper coins dropped by old
    women
Into the alms-boxes of venerable churches.

AFTER A STORM

You walk under the ice trees.
They sway, and crackle,
And arch themselves splendidly
To deck your going.
The white sun flips them into colour
Before you.
They are blue,
And mauve,
And emerald.
They are amber,
And jade,
And sardonyx.
They are silver fretted to flame
And startled to stillness,
Bunched, splintered, iridescent.
You walk under the ice trees
And the bright snow creaks as you step upon it.
My dogs leap about you,
And their barking strikes upon the air
Like sharp hammer-strokes on metal.
You walk under the ice trees
But you are more dazzling than the ice flowers,
And the dogs' barking
Is not so loud to me as your quietness.
You walk under the ice trees
At ten o'clock in the morning.

ANTICIPATION

I have been temperate always,
But I am like to be very drunk
With your coming.
There have been times
I feared to walk down the street
Lest I should reel with the wine of you,
And jerk against my neighbours
As they go by.
I am parched now, and my tongue is horrible in my
    mouth,
But my brain is noisy
With the clash and gurgle of filling wine-cups.

PATIENCE

Be patient with you?
   When the stooping sky
Leans down upon the hills
And tenderly, as one who soothing stills
   An anguish, gathers earth to lie
Embraced and girdled. Do the sun-filled men
   Feel patience then?

Be patient with you?
   When the snow-girt earth
Cracks to let through a spurt
Of sudden green, and from the muddy dirt
   A snowdrop leaps, how mark its worth
To eyes frost-hardened, and do weary men
   Feel patience then?

Be patient with you?
   When pain's iron bars
Their rivets tighten, stern
To bend and break their victims; as they turn,
   Hopeless, there stand the purple jars
Of night to spill oblivion. Do these men
   Feel patience then?

Be patient with you?
    You! My sun and moon!
My basketful of flowers!
My money-bag of shining dreams! My hours,
    Windless and still, of afternoon!
You are my world and I your citizen.
    What meaning can have patience then?

A SPRIG OF ROSEMARY

I cannot see your face.
When I think of you,
It is your hands which I see.
Your hands
Sewing,
Holding a book,
Resting for a moment on the sill of a window.
My eyes keep always the sight of your hands,
But my heart holds the sound of your voice,
And the soft brightness which is your soul.

SUMMER

Some men there are who find in nature all
Their inspiration, hers the sympathy
Which spurs them on to any great endeavor,
To them the fields and woods are closest friends,
And they hold dear communion with the hills;
The voice of waters soothes them with its fall,
And the great winds bring healing in their sound.
To them a city is a prison house
Where pent up human forces labour and strive,
Where beauty dwells not, driven forth by man;
But where in winter they must live until
Summer gives back the spaces of the hills.
To me it is not so. I love the earth
And all the gifts of her so lavish hand:
Sunshine and flowers, rivers and rushing winds,
Thick branches swaying in a winter storm,
And moonlight playing in a boat's wide wake;
But more than these, and much, ah, how much more,
I love the very human heart of man.
Above me spreads the hot, blue mid-day sky,
Far down the hillside lies the sleeping lake
Lazily reflecting back the sun,
And scarcely ruffled by the little breeze
Which wanders idly through the nodding ferns.
The blue crest of the distant mountain, tops
The green crest of the hill on which I sit;

And it is summer, glorious, deep-toned summer,
The very crown of nature's changing year
When all her surging life is at its full.
To me alone it is a time of pause,
A void and silent space between two worlds,
When inspiration lags, and feeling sleeps,
Gathering strength for efforts yet to come.
For life alone is creator of life,
And closest contact with the human world
Is like a lantern shining in the night
To light me to a knowledge of myself.
I love the vivid life of winter months
In constant intercourse with human minds,
When every new experience is gain
And on all sides we feel the great world's heart;
The pulse and throb of life which makes us men!

BY MESSENGER

One night
When there was a clear moon,
I sat down
To write a poem
About maple-trees.
But the dazzle of moonlight
In the ink
Blinded me,
And I could only write
What I remembered.
Therefore, on the wrapping of my poem
I have inscribed your name.

AFTERMATH

I learnt to write to you in happier days,
    And every letter was a piece I chipped
    From off my heart, a fragment newly clipped
From the mosaic of life; its blues and grays,
Its throbbing reds, I gave to earn your praise.
    To make a pavement for your feet I stripped
    My soul for you to walk upon, and slipped
Beneath your steps to soften all your ways.
    But now my letters are like blossoms pale
We strew upon a grave with hopeless tears.
    I ask no recompense, I shall not fail
Although you do not heed; the long, sad years
    Still pass, and still I scatter flowers frail,
And whisper words of love which no one hears.

MORNING SONG, WITH DRUMS

The pheasants cry in the dawn,
Mocking the glitter of the nearby city
Struck upon the sky.

Ivy *in a wind,*
   Smooth grass,
      Old cedar-trees.

Change is a bitter thing to contemplate
Across a grey dawn.
Puff-ball world, forsooth
A kick and it is broken into smoke.

The pheasant's cry is raucous
   in the dawn.

MIRAGE

How is it that, being gone, you fill my days,
    And all the long nights are made glad by thee?
    No loneliness is this, nor misery,
But great content that these should be the ways
Whereby the Fancy, dreaming as she strays,
    Makes bright and present what she would would be.
    And who shall say if the reality
Is not with dreams so pregnant. For delays
    And hindrances may bar the wished-for end;
A thousand misconceptions may prevent
    Our souls from coming near enough to blend;
Let me but think we have the same intent,
    That each one needs to call the other, "friend!"
It may be vain illusion. I'm content.

AUTUMN

All day I have watched the purple vine leaves
Fall into the water.
And now in the moonlight they still fall,
But each leaf is fringed with silver.

SOLITAIRE

When night drifts along the streets of the
    city,
And sifts down between the uneven roofs,
My mind begins to peek and peer.
It plays at ball in old, blue Chinese
    gardens,
And shakes wrought dice-cups in Pagan
    temples
Amid the broken flutings of white pillars.
It dances with purple and yellow crocuses
    in its hair,
And its feet shine as they flutter over
    drenched grasses.
How light and laughing my mind is,
When all the good folk have put out
    their bedroom candles,
And the city is still!

FIREWORKS

You hate me and I hate you,
And we are so polite, we two!

But whenever I see you, I burst apart
And scatter the sky with my blazing heart.
It spits and sparkles in stars and balls,
Buds into roses—and flares, and falls.

Scarlet buttons, and pale green disks,
Silver spirals and asterisks,
Shoot and tremble in a mist
Peppered with mauve and amethyst.

I shine in the windows and light up the trees,
And all because I hate you, if you please.

And when you meet me, you rend asunder
And go up in a flaming wonder
Of saffron cubes, and crimson moons,
And wheels all amaranths and maroons.

Golden lozenges and spades,
Arrows of malachites and jades,
Patens of copper, azure sheaves.
As you mount, you flash in the glossy leaves.
Such fireworks as we make, we two!
Because you hate me and I hate you.

THE LITTLE GARDEN

A little garden on a bleak hillside
    Where deep the heavy, dazzling mountain snow
    Lies far into the spring. The sun's pale glow
Is scarcely able to melt patches wide
About the single rose bush. All denied
    Of nature's tender ministries. But no, —
    For wonder-working faith has made it blow
With flowers many hued and starry-eyed.
    Here sleeps the sun long, idle summer hours;
Here butterflies and bees fare far to rove
    Amid the crumpled leaves of poppy flowers;
Here four o'clocks, to the passionate night above
    Fling whiffs of perfume, like pale incense showers.
A little garden, loved with a great love!

DAWN ADVENTURE

I stood in my window
    looking at the double cherry:
A great height of white stillness,
Underneath a sky
    the colour of milky grey jade.
Suddenly a crow flew between me
  and the tree—
Swooping, falling, in a shadow-black
  curve—
And blotted himself out in the blurred
  branches
    of a leafless ash.
There he stayed for some time,
    and I could only distinguish him
      by his slight moving.
Then a wind caught the upper branches
  of the cherry,
And the long, white stems nodded up
  and down,
    casually, to me in the window,
Nodded—but overhead the grey jade
  clouds
    passed slowly, indifferently, to-
    ward the sea.

THE LETTER

Little cramped words scrawling all over
   the paper
Like draggled fly's legs,
What can you tell of the flaring moon
Through the oak leaves?
Or of my uncurtained window
   and the bare floor
Spattered with moonlight?
Your silly quirks and twists have nothing
   in them
Of blossoming hawthorns,
And this paper is dull, crisp, smooth,
   virgin of loveliness
Beneath my hand.

I am tired, Beloved, of chafing my heart
   against
The want of you;
Of squeezing it into little inkdrops,
And posting it.
And I scald alone, here, under the fire
Of the great moon.

VERNAL EQUINOX

The scent of hyacinths, like a pale mist, lies
   between me and my book;
And the South Wind, washing through the room,
Makes the candles quiver.
My nerves sting at a spatter of rain on the shutter,
And I am uneasy with the thrusting of green shoots
Outside, in the night.

Why are you not here to overpower me with your
   tense and urgent love?

SPRING DAY

Bath

The day is fresh-washed and fair, and there is a
smell of tulips and narcissus in the air.

The sunshine pours in at the bathroom window
and bores through the water in the bath-tub in
lathes and planes of greenish-white. It cleaves
the water into flaws like a jewel, and cracks it
to bright light.

Little spots of sunshine lie on the surface of
the water and dance, dance, and their reflections
wobble deliciously over the ceiling; a stir of my
finger sets them whirring, reeling. I move a foot,
and the planes of light in the water jar. I lie
back and laugh, and let the green-white water,
the sun-flawed beryl water, flow over me. The
day is almost too bright to bear, the green water
covers me from the too bright day. I will lie
here awhile and play with the water and the sun
spots.

The sky is blue and high. A crow flaps by the
window, and there is a whiff of tulips and narcissus in the air.

Lilacs,
False blue,
White,
Purple,
Colour of lilac.
Heart-leaves of lilac all over New England,
Roots of lilac under all the soil of New England,
Lilac in me because I am New England,
Because my roots are in it,
Because my leaves are of it,
Because my flowers are for it,
Because it is my country
And I speak to it of itself
And sing of it with my own voice
Since certainly it is mine.

STUPIDITY

Dearest, forgive that with my clumsy touch
   I broke and bruised your rose.
   I hardly could suppose
It were a thing so fragile that my clutch
     Could kill it, thus.

It stood so proudly up upon its stem,
   I knew no thought of fear,
   And coming very near
Fell, overbalanced, to your garment's hem,
     Tearing it down.

Now, stooping, I gather, one by one,
   The crimson petals, all
   Outspread about my fall.
They hold their fragrance still, a blood-red cone
     Of memory.

And with my words I carve a little jar
   To keep their scented dust,
   Which, opening, you must
Breathe to your soul, and, breathing, know me far
     More grieved than you.

VICARIOUS

When I stand under the willow-tree
Above the river,
In my straw-coloured silken garment
Embroidered with purple chrysanthemums,
It is not at the bright water
That I am gazing,
But at your portrait,
Which I have caused to be painted
On my fan.

A DECADE

When you came, you were like red wine and honey,
And the taste of you burnt my mouth with its sweetness.
Now you are like morning bread,
Smooth and pleasant.
I hardly taste you at all for I know your savour,
But I am completely nourished.

A GIFT

See! I give myself to you, Beloved!
My words are little jars
For you to take and put upon a shelf.
Their shapes are quaint and beautiful,
And they have many pleasant colours and lustres
To recommend them.
Also the scent from them fills the room
With sweetness of flowers and crushed grasses.

When I shall have given you the last one,
You will have the whole of me,
But I shall be dead.

THE GIVER OF STARS

Hold your soul open for my welcoming.
Let the quiet of your spirit bathe me
With its clear and rippled coolness,
That, loose-limbed and weary, I find rest,
Outstretched upon your peace, as on a bed of ivory.

Let the flickering flame of your soul play all
                about me,
That into my limbs may come the keenness of fire,
The life and joy of tongues of flame,
And, going out from you, tightly strung
                and in tune,
I may rouse the blear-eyed world,
And pour into it the beauty which you have begotten.

SHORE GRASS

The moon is cold over the sand-dunes,
And the clumps of sea-grasses flow and glitter;
The thin chime of my watch tells the quarter
    after midnight;
And still I hear nothing
But the windy beating of the sea.

CROWNED

You came to me bearing bright roses,
    Red like the wine of your heart;
You twisted them into a garland
    To set me aside from the mart.
Red roses to crown me your lover,
    And I walked aureoled and apart.

Enslaved and encircled, I bore it,
    Proud token of my gift to you.
The petals waned paler, and shriveled,
    And dropped; and the thorns started through.
Bitter thorns to proclaim me your lover,
    A diadem woven with rue.

SPRING LONGING

The South wind blows open the folds
    of my dress,
My feet leave wet tracks in the earth
    of my garden,
The willows along the canal sing
      with new leaves turned
      upon the wind.
I walk along the tow-path
Gazing at the level water.
Should I see a ribbed edge
Running upon its clearness,
I should know that this was caused
By the prow of the boat
In which you are to return.

WHITE AND GREEN

Hey! My daffodil-crowned,
Slim and without sandals!
As the sudden spurt of flame upon darkness
So my eyeballs are startled with you,
Supple-limbed youth among the fruit-trees,
Light runner through tasselled orchards.
You are an almond flower unsheathed
Leaping and flickering between the budded branches.

PATTERNS

I walk down the garden paths,
And all the daffodils
Are blowing, and the bright blue squills.
I walk down the patterned garden-paths
In my stiff, brocaded gown.
With my powdered hair and jewelled fan,
I too am a rare
Pattern. As I wander down
The garden paths.

My dress is richly figured,
And the train
Makes a pink and silver stain
On the gravel, and the thrift
Of the borders.
Just a plate of current fashion
Tripping by in high-heeled, ribboned shoes.
Not a softness anywhere about me,
Only whalebone and brocade.
And I sink on a seat in the shade
Of a lime tree. For my passion

Wars against

Wars against the stiff brocade.
The daffodils and squills
Flutter in the breeze
As they please.
And I weep;
For the lime tree is in blossom
And one small flower has dropped upon my bosom.

And the splashing of waterdrops
In the marble fountain
Comes down the garden-paths.
The dripping never stops.
Underneath my stiffened gown
Is the softness of a woman bathing in a marble basin,
A basin in the midst of hedges grown
So thick, she cannot see her lover hiding,
But she guesses he is near,
And the sliding of the water
Seems the stroking of a dear
Hand upon her.
What is Summer in a fine brocaded gown!
I should like to see it lying in a heap upon the ground.
All the pink and silver crumpled up on the ground.

I would be the pink and silver as I ran along the paths,
And he would stumble after,
Bewildered by my laughter.
I should see the sun flashing from his sword-hilt
    and buckles on his shoes.
I would choose
To lead him in a maze along the patterned paths,
A bright and laughing maze for my heavy-booted lover.
Till he caught me in the shade,
And the buttons of his waistcoat bruised my body
    as he clasped me,
Aching, melting, unafraid.
With the shadows of the leaves and the sundrops,
And the plopping of the waterdrops,
All about us in the open afternoon—
I am very like to swoon
With the weight of this brocade,
For the sun sifts through the shade.

Underneath the fallen blossom
In my bosom,
Is a letter I have hid.
It was brought to me this morning by a rider from
    the Duke.

                              "Madam, we

"Madam, we regret to inform you that Lord Hartwell
Died in action Thursday se'nnight."
As I read it in the white, morning sunlight,
The letters squirmed like snakes.
"Any answer, Madam," said my footman.
"No," I told him.
"See that the messenger takes some refreshment.
No, no answer."
And I walked into the garden,
Up and down the patterned paths,
In my stiff, correct brocade.
The blue and yellow flowers stood up proudly
   in the sun,
Each one.
I stood upright too,
Held rigid to the pattern
By the stiffness of my gown.
Up and down I walked.
Up and down.

In a month he would have been my husband.
In a month, here, underneath this lime,
We would have broken the pattern;
He for me, and I for him,
He as Colonel, I as Lady,
On this shady seat.

He had a whim
That sunlight carried blessing.
And I answered, "It shall be as you have said."
Now he is dead.

In Summer and in Winter I shall walk
Up and down
The patterned garden-paths
In my stiff, brocaded gown.
The squills and daffodils
Will give place to pillared roses, and to asters,
    and to snow.
I shall go
Up and down,
In my gown.
Gorgeously arrayed,
Boned and stayed.
And the softness of my body will be guarded
    from embrace
By each button, hook, and lace.
For the man who should loose me is dead,
Fighting with the Duke in Flanders,
In a pattern called a war.
Christ! What are patterns for?

Printed on Hallmark Eggshell Book paper.
Set in Romanee, a 20-th century typeface designed
by Jan van Krimpen of Holland. Romanee was
created to accompany the only surviving italic of
the 17-th century typefounder Christoffel Van Dijck.